THIS BOOK BELONGS TO:

To Callahan Lou, always dream BIG and love BIGGER.

Copyright © 2018 by Shelby Florenz

All rights reserved. No part of this publication may be reproduced, distributed, or transmitted in any form or by any means, including photocopying, recording, or other electronic or mechanical methods, without the prior written permission of the publisher, except in the case of brief quotations embodied in critical reviews and certain other noncommercial uses permitted by copyright law. For permission requests, write to the publisher, addressed "Attention: Permissions Coordinator," at the address below.

ISBN: 978-0-692-09286-6 (Hardcover)

Any references to historical events, real people, or real places are used fictitiously. Names, characters, and places are products of the author's imagination.

Front cover and all illustrations by Dakotah Archer
Book design by Dakotah Archer

GUANGZHOU YIXING PRINTING PRODUCTS CO. LTD.
Printed in China

First printing edition 2018.

Sincerely Santa
105 Sanchez Drive West
Ponte Vedra, FL 32082

www.shopsincerelysanta.com

"I believe the spirit of Christmas is enough to change the world."

Written by Shelby Florenz

Illustrated and designed by Dakotah Archer

Merry Christmas my children, Merry Christmas to all!
It is that time of year when our duty calls.
While I'm out and about making wishes come true,
I've left you a list of things we can do!

The best gift we can give is completing each goal,
spreading holiday cheer twelve days in a row.
Good luck my children, I know you will do great!
After finishing the book, something beautiful awaits.

The first day of twelve I ask for only a little;
Send a song to a loved one, a poem or a riddle.
So simple and yet, we can bring them a smile,
So pick out a tune and dance for a while!

Our moms and our dads deserve more than day two,
But let us start here, with a million Thank You's.
Then give them a day they will remember forever,
Give them their own BEST DAY EVER!

Day three is my favorite, or one of them, at least.
Today is the day we give someone a feast!
Maybe a feast, or a snack, or maybe bake some cookies.
Let's give them a treat or some kind of goody.

Today is day four and for our four legged friends.
Today we should play with them for hours on end.
Every day they are there when you walk in the door,
Every day they give you love, today you give them yours.

Day five of Christmas is to lift up the sick.
Can you make them smile with a joke or a trick?
Sometimes the best gift of all is the time that you spend
Taking care of one another with the hand that you lend.

Day six is to help the world if you choose;
Remember to reduce, recycle, and reuse.
Our Creator made us a planet perfectly green,
Now it is up to us to keep it fresh and so clean.

Day seven is for our sisters and brothers.
Who would we be without one another?
Tell them you love them, make the phone call.
It is them who have your back
When your back's against the wall.

You've made it to day eight, and that's the day of the brave.
Make someone feel something they cannot explain.
Stand up to a bully, be kind, and do good;
Be courageous for the kid that is misunderstood.

9

Day nine is for singing the songs I love most.
Today is the day for the big Christmas boast.
Let them hear you sing songs of laughter and cheer,
We only get to do this one month of the year!

10

The tenth day of Christmas, be committed to love all.
Whether they're happy or sad, short or tall.
The people hardest to love need it the most!
Let's spread our love from coast to coast.

Day eleven is world changing, I hope you take action!
Today I want you to create a chain reaction.
It starts with some kindness and then you pass it along,
As the circle gets bigger, our world becomes strong.

12

Day twelve is here, I cannot thank you enough!
I know my list is long and often can be tough.
So today is for you, I hope you find yourself proud
Of all the good you've done and all the love you've found.

As you finish this book, I hope now you can see
The best gifts of all aren't under the tree.
You've brought magic and love and joy to this place,
Which leaves my heart full and a smile on my face.

20____ Write on your list what you've done for each day!

Day 1 _____

Day 2 _____

Day 3 _____

Day 4 _____

Day 5 _____

Day 6 _____

Day 7 _____

Day 8 _____

Day 9 _____

Day 10 _____

Day 11 _____

Day 12 _____

20____   Write on your list what you've done for each day!

Day 1 _____   Day 7 _____

_____   _____

Day 2 _____   Day 8 _____

_____   _____

Day 3 _____   Day 9 _____

_____   _____

Day 4 _____   Day 10 _____

_____   _____

Day 5 _____   Day 11 _____

_____   _____

Day 6 _____   Day 12 _____

_____   _____

20____   Write on your list what you've done for each day!

Day 1 _____

Day 2 _____

Day 3 _____

Day 4 _____

Day 5 _____

Day 6 _____

Day 7 _____

Day 8 _____

Day 9 _____

Day 10 _____

Day 11 _____

Day 12 _____

20____   Write on your list what you've done for each day!

Day 1 _____

_____

Day 2 _____

_____

Day 3 _____

_____

Day 4 _____

_____

Day 5 _____

_____

Day 6 _____

_____

Day 7 _____

_____

Day 8 _____

_____

Day 9 _____

_____

Day 10 _____

_____

Day 11 _____

_____

Day 12 _____

_____

20____   Write on your list what you've done for each day!

Day 1 _____   Day 7 _____

_____   _____

Day 2 _____   Day 8 _____

_____   _____

Day 3 _____   Day 9 _____

_____   _____

Day 4 _____   Day 10 _____

_____   _____

Day 5 _____   Day 11 _____

_____   _____

Day 6 _____   Day 12 _____

_____   _____

20____ Write on your list what you've done for each day!

Day 1 _____

Day 2 _____

Day 3 _____

Day 4 _____

Day 5 _____

Day 6 _____

Day 7 _____

Day 8 _____

Day 9 _____

Day 10 _____

Day 11 _____

Day 12 _____

20____   Write on your list what you've done for each day!

Day 1 _____

Day 2 _____

Day 3 _____

Day 4 _____

Day 5 _____

Day 6 _____

Day 7 _____

Day 8 _____

Day 9 _____

Day 10 _____

Day 11 _____

Day 12 _____